Ninja Foodi 2-Basket Air Fryer Cookbook for Beginners

1000-Day Ninja Air Fryer Recipes for Faster, Healthier & Crispier Fried Favorites | Fry, Broil, Roast & Bake Most Wanted Family Meals

Dorth Vanikam

Table of Contents

Introduction

Cardiovascular disease remains one of the leading causes of mortality all over the world. High cholesterol from a poor diet has largely contributed to heart problems and other complications. As more people are gearing towards a healthier lifestyle, their habits and behaviors also shift. Since diet has a great impact on overall health, people are becoming more intentional not only in terms of food selection but also how their food is prepared and cooked.

An increasing number of people are upgrading to more compact multi-cookers for their numerous benefits. One such appliance that has become so trendy is the air fryer. Air fryers are similar to convection ovens since they cook using hot air that is circulated inside a chamber. Air fryers have become a favorite among health-conscious individuals since it uses much less oil than traditional cookers. Air fryers can make delicious meals with less time and effort, making them a more desirable option for daily cooking.

Chapter 1: An Overview

Ninja Foodi is one of the leading brands when it comes to air fryers. Although it manufactures several home appliances such as pressure cookers and toasters, its air fryers are among consumer favorites. Its latest air fryer with an 8-quart capacity has two baskets that can cook two different foods simultaneously. Each zone or basket that has a 4-quart capacity is equipped with its heating element and fan. Its proprietary DualZone Technology on the DZ201 model provides us with unique features such as the Smart Finish and Match Cook.

Smart Finish allows you to set different cooking functions, times, and temperatures for each dish and have them finish at the same time. The Match Cook option allows you to automatically use the same settings for both baskets. Unlike single compartment air fryers, you will be able to cook twice the food in less time with Ninja Foodi's latest air fryer model. It also has six cooking functions: air fry, roast, air broil, bake, dehydrate and reheat. The DZ201 can reach a maximum temperature of 450 degrees Fahrenheit, letting you cook a wide variety of dishes.

How to Operate the Ninja DZ201 Foodi 6-in-1 2-Basket Air Fryer

Before cooking with your air fryer for the first time, take out all packaging materials and labels. Clean the fryer baskets and crisper plates using hot water and soap. Make sure that these components are thoroughly dried before putting them back in the main unit.

To get started, connect your air fryer to an electrical outlet and press the power button. Since Ninja Foodi's DZ201 model is the very first air fryer that has two baskets, it also comes with some neat presets that will bring more convenience to your cooking.

The air fryer settings default to zone 1. To use the Smart Finish option, place the food in the first basket, and select the cooking program. Next, adjust the time and temperature using the up and down arrow buttons. Select zone 2 and place food on the second basket. Choose the cooking program and set the desired time and temperature. Press the Smart Finish button, then the Start/Pause button to initiate the cooking process. Take note that if the air broil function is already used in zone 1, it will not be available to use for zone 2.

If you don't need the Smart Finish function but would still use both baskets, simply follow the steps mentioned above and skip pressing the Smart Finish button. This will allow you to start the programs simultaneously and finish on the individually set cooking times.

To use the Match Cook option, place food in the baskets, and select the cooking function. Set the time and temperature using the arrow buttons. Press the Match Cook option, then the Start/Pause button to initiate the process.

To use a single zone for cooking, select the desired cooking program, time, and temperature. Then press the Start/Pause button to begin cooking.

Tap the power button to turn the air fryer off. Unplug the unit by firmly holding the plug and gently pulling it away from the electrical outlet. Never yank the cord when unplugging to avoid causing damage.

Safety Guidelines

It is very tempting to get right into cooking when you see your air fryer for the first time. We've all been there. But remember that it is always a best practice to read the manual first before operating any appliance to ensure safety.

- Read and follow the user's manual to ensure safety while operating the appliance.
- Ensure that only individuals who have read the guide and are fit to operate the appliance should use it.
- Do not let children and persons with reduced capabilities operate the appliance without the close supervision of a responsible adult.
- Never let children play with the air fryer.
- Always exercise caution when using the appliance, especially when children are around.
- Never put the appliance near heated surfaces such as ovens and burners. Similarly, keep it away from wet or damp areas.
- Position the air fryer on a level and heat-resistant surface, leaving at least six inches of space all around the body.
- Do not move or transfer the air fryer while it is in operation.
- Make sure that the air intake vent and air outlet are unobstructed to prevent any

damage and accidents.

- Do not place flammable materials near the air fryer.
- Never immerse the unit, cord, and plug in water or any type of liquid.
- Avoid using an extension cord with this appliance. The unit is intentionally fitted with a short electrical cord to prevent tripping and similar accidents.
- Make sure that the basket and crisper plates are completely dry before placing them back into the main unit.
- Only use the components provided by the manufacturers. Do not use attachments or accessories that are not recommended or produced by SharkNinja.
- Do not connect this unit with an external timer or remote-control device.
- Do not place hot baskets on top of the appliance or on surfaces that are not heat-resistant.
- Never put anything on top of the appliance at all times.
- Never use these baskets with an oven, microwave, burner, grill, and similar appliances. The baskets are not intended for use in deep frying.
- Before pressing the start button or operating the unit, make sure that the baskets and all other components are installed correctly and securely.
- Never use the air fryer without the baskets attached.
- Be careful when handling heated surfaces. Use oven mitts, insulated gloves, or dish towels when taking out food from the appliance to avoid any burns.
- The air fryer is intended for indoor and household use only. Operating the appliance apart from its intended use by the manufacturers may cause injury or damage to property.
- Do not let the power cord hang as it may cause accidents. Use a wall socket that is located above the counter.
- Do not operate the air fryer if you notice any damage to any of its parts, particularly with the cord and plug. If the unit malfunctions, unplug immediately and get in touch with the Ninja Foodi customer service.
- Immediately unplug the unit if you see any black smoke coming from the air fryer. Wait until the smoke subsides before taking out the baskets or other parts.
- Always unplug the unit after each use and before cleaning.

Tips for Cooking Success

Remember these nifty tips whenever you are cooking with your new air fryer.

- Pressing the Start/Pause button while using the Smart Finish will pause the cooking process on both zones. Press the same button to resume cooking.
- If at any time you need to pause the cooking process in one of the baskets, first select the zone, then the Start/Pause button.
- To stop or end the cooking process, select the zone, then set the time to zero using the arrow down button. The display should show End after a few seconds, and the cooking process in this zone will stop.
- You can adjust the temperature and time in each zone at any time during the cooking process. Select the zone, then adjust the setting using the arrow buttons.
- Place a single layer of food and avoid stacking whenever possible.
- To get the best results, toss or shake the food at least twice within the cooking cycle, especially for foods that overlap, like French fries. This will produce a more even cooking throughout.
- When cooking fresh vegetables, add at least one tablespoon of cooking oil. More oil can be added to create a crispier texture.
- Use the crisper plates when you want your food to become crunchy. Note that the crisper plates will slightly elevate your food to allow hot air to permeate the bottom and result in a crispier texture.
- Follow the correct breading technique for wet battered food. Coat the food with flour first, then with egg, and finally with bread crumbs. Press the crumbs into the food to avoid it from flying around when air frying.
- It is best to regularly check the progress to avoid overcooking. Refer to the cooking chart for different foods in the quick start guide included in the package.
- A food-safe temperature must be reached to avoid any foodborne illness. Use a thermometer to check for doneness, especially when cooking raw meat. Instant-read thermometers are your best choice for this.
- Once cooking time is up or when the desired browning is achieved, promptly remove the food from the unit.
- Do not use metal cutleries or tools that can damage the non-stick coating. Dump the

food directly on a plate or use silicon-tipped tongs.

- Small bits of food may be blown away while cooking. You can avoid this by securing pieces of food with toothpicks.
- To cook recipes intended for traditional ovens, simply reduce the temperature by 25 degrees Fahrenheit and regularly check for doneness.
- Do not let food touch the heating elements.
- Never overload the baskets. Not only will this result in uneven cooking, but it may also cause the appliance to malfunction as well.
- The quick start guide provides useful information like cooking charts for various foods, tasty meals to make using the Smart Finish function, and other delightful recipes to easily try with the Ninja Foodi 6-in-1 air fryer.

Tips for Cleaning and Maintenance

To keep the unit in an excellent working state, always make sure that you follow the manufacturer's guidelines on how to properly clean and maintain the air fryer.

Remember to follow these easy tips.

- Always unplug and clean the unit after use.
- Let the air fryer completely cool down before cleaning.
- The crisper plates and baskets are all dishwasher-safe. They may also be cleaned by hand using warm soapy water. Ideally, the baskets should be hand-washed to maintain their coating.
- Never scrape or use any abrasive cleaners on the crisper plates and baskets. If there is baked-on food, soak the components in warm soapy water until it can be removed easily.
- The main body is neither dishwasher-safe nor water-resistant. Never soak the main body and electrical cord in water or any form of liquid.
- Wipe the exterior using a clean, damp cloth.
- Regularly check the appliance for signs of damage.

Chapter 2: Breakfast and Brunch Recipes

Sweet Potato Hash

Preparation Time: 20 minutes
Cooking Time: 15 minutes
Servings: 4

Ingredients:

- 1 onion, chopped
- 1 bell pepper, diced
- 3 sweet potatoes, diced
- 2 tablespoons olive oil
- ½ teaspoon dried thyme
- ½ teaspoon ground cinnamon
- ½ teaspoon ground nutmeg
- Salt and pepper to taste

Method:

1. Toss veggies in olive oil.
2. Season with herbs, spices, salt and pepper.
3. Add to the air fryer basket of the Ninja DZ201 Foodi.
4. Choose air fry setting.
5. Set it to 350 degrees F for 15 minutes.

Serving Suggestions: Serve with fried eggs.

Preparation & Cooking Tips: Cook longer if you want the sweet potatoes more tender.

Pumpkin French Toast

Preparation Time: 10 minutes
Cooking Time: 5 minutes
Servings: 1

Ingredients:

- 4 slices bread
- ¾ cup milk
- 4 eggs, beaten
- ½ cup pumpkin puree
- 1 teaspoon vanilla extract
- 2 tablespoons brown sugar
- ½ teaspoon ground ginger
- ½ teaspoon ground nutmeg
- ½ teaspoon ground cinnamon

Method:

1. Add all ingredients except bread to a bowl.
2. Mix well.
3. Soak bread in the mixture for 30 seconds.
4. Add the bread to the air fryer basket.
5. Set it to air fry.
6. Cook at 320 degrees F for 5 minutes.
7. Flip and cook another 5 minutes.

Serving Suggestions: Sprinkle with cinnamon before serving.

Preparation & Cooking Tips: Use whole wheat bread if available.

Strawberry Croissant French Toast

Preparation Time: 10 minutes
Cooking Time: 15 minutes
Servings: 4

Ingredients:

- 6 croissants, sliced in half
- 2 cups strawberries, diced
- 8 oz. cream cheese, diced
- 1 cup milk
- 6 eggs, beaten
- 1 teaspoon vanilla extract
- ¼ cup honey
- Salt to taste

Method:

1. Add the croissant to the air fryer basket.
2. Spread strawberries and cream cheese on top.
3. In a bowl, mix milk, eggs, vanilla, honey and salt.
4. Pour this mixture on top of the croissants.
5. Choose air fry setting.
6. Cook at 320 degrees F for 20 minutes.

Serving Suggestions: Serve with a cup of coffee or milk.

Preparation & Cooking Tips: Thaw first if using frozen croissants.

Ricotta Toasted with Tomatoes, Walnuts & Roasted Garlic

Preparation Time: 10 minutes
Cooking Time: 10 minutes
Servings: 2

Ingredients:

- 2 tablespoons olive oil
- 1 clove garlic, diced
- 1 cup cherry tomatoes, sliced in half
- ¼ cup walnuts, diced
- Salt and pepper to taste
- 2 slices bread
- ½ cup ricotta cheese
- 2 tablespoons Parmesan cheese, shredded

Method:

1. In a bowl, combine oil, garlic, tomatoes, walnuts, salt and pepper.
2. Add mixture to the air fryer basket.
3. Set it to air fry.
4. Cook at 330 degrees F for 5 minutes.
5. Add the bread to the other basket.
6. Set it to 330 degrees F for 3 minutes.
7. Spread the ricotta cheese on the toasted bread.
8. Top with the garlic mixture and Parmesan cheese.

Serving Suggestions: Garnish with chopped parsley.

Preparation & Cooking Tips: Use wheat bread if available.

Zucchini Bread

Preparation Time: 20 minutes
Cooking Time: 30 minutes
Servings: 4

Ingredients:

Dry

- 3 cups all-purpose flour
- 1 teaspoon baking powder
- 1 teaspoon baking soda
- 1 teaspoon allspice
- 1 teaspoon ground nutmeg
- 1 teaspoon ground cinnamon
- 1 teaspoon salt

Wet

- 3 eggs, beaten
- 1 cup vegetable oil
- 2 cups zucchini, grated
- 1 cup walnuts, diced
- 2 ¼ cup sugar
- 1 teaspoon vanilla extract

Method:

1. In a bowl, mix the dry ingredients.
2. In another bowl, combine the wet ingredients.
3. Add second bowl to the first one.
4. Add mixture to a small loaf pan.
5. Place the loaf pan in the air fryer basket.
6. Set it to air fry.
7. Cook at 320 degrees F for 30 minutes.

Serving Suggestions: Let cool for 10 minutes before slicing and serving.

Preparation & Cooking Tips: Squeeze zucchini dry before using.

Bacon Quiche Tarts

Preparation Time: 15 minutes
Cooking Time: 20 minutes
Servings: 8

Ingredients:

- 2 eggs
- 5 teaspoons milk
- 6 oz. cream cheese
- ½ cup Colby cheese, shredded
- 1 tablespoon onion, chopped
- 2 tablespoons green bell pepper, chopped
- 8 oz. refrigerated crescent rolls, separated into triangles
- 5 slices bacon, cooked and crumbled

Method:

1. Beat eggs in a bowl.
2. Stir in milk, cream cheese, Colby cheese, onion, and green bell pepper.
3. Press crescent triangles into muffin cups.
4. Add egg mixture to the muffin cups.
5. Sprinkle with bacon.
6. Place muffin cups inside the air fryer basket.
7. Choose bake setting.
8. Cook at 375 degrees F for 25 minutes.

Serving Suggestions: Garnish with chopped green onion.

Preparation & Cooking Tips: You can use nondairy milk like almond milk for this recipe.

Egg & Spinach Pizza

Preparation Time: 20 minutes
Cooking Time: 15 minutes
Servings: 4

Ingredients:

- 1 refrigerated pizza crust
- 5 oz. baby spinach
- 1 tablespoon olive oil.
- ¼ cup Parmesan cheese, grated
- 3 tablespoons sour cream
- 1 clove garlic, minced
- Salt and pepper to taste
- 4 eggs

Method:

1. Slice the pizza crust into 4 to fit inside the air fryer basket.
2. In a pan over medium heat, cook spinach in olive oil.
3. Add spinach to a bowl.
4. Stir in the remaining ingredients except the eggs.
5. Spread spinach mixture on top of pizza crust.
6. Crack the egg on top.
7. Place it inside the air fryer basket.
8. Set it to bake.
9. Bake at 350 degrees F for 10 minutes.

Serving Suggestions: Sprinkle with Parmesan cheese before serving.

Preparation & Cooking Tips: You can also make your own pizza crust if you like.

Baked Oatmeal

Preparation Time: 10 minutes
Cooking Time: 25 minutes
Servings: 4

Ingredients:

- 1 ½ cups quick-cooking oats
- 1 egg, beaten
- ½ cup milk
- ¼ cup butter, melted
- ½ cup sugar
- 1 teaspoon baking powder
- 1 teaspoon vanilla extract
- ¾ teaspoon salt

Method:

1. Combine all the ingredients in an air fryer safe bowl.
2. Stir well.
3. Place in the air fryer basket.
4. Set it to bake.
5. Cook at 350 degrees F for 30 minutes.

Serving Suggestions: Serve with fresh fruits and warm milk.

Preparation & Cooking Tips: You can also use rolled oats but cook for a few more minutes.

Frittata with Broccoli, Tomatoes & Goat Cheese

Preparation Time: 25 minutes

Cooking Time: 15 minutes

Servings: 4

Ingredients:

- 8 eggs
- Salt and pepper to taste
- ½ onion, chopped
- 1 tomato, chopped
- 2 cups broccoli florets
- 1 tablespoon olive oil
- 1 oz. goat cheese

Method:

1. Beat eggs, salt and pepper in a bowl.
2. Add this to the air fryer basket.
3. Set it to broil.
4. Cook for 3 minutes.
5. Toss the onion, tomato and broccoli in oil and add to the other air fryer basket.
6. Set it to air fry.
7. Cook at 350 degrees F for 5 minutes or until broccoli is tender enough.
8. Top the eggs with the tomato mixture and goat cheese.

Serving Suggestions: Slice into four and serve.

Preparation & Cooking Tips: You can also add goat cheese to the egg mixture instead of using it as topping.

Cheesy Potatoes

Preparation Time: 10 minutes
Cooking Time: 45 minutes
Servings: 4

Ingredients:

- 6 potatoes, sliced into cubes
- 1 onion, chopped
- 1 teaspoon paprika
- 1 teaspoon dried oregano
- 2 tablespoons olive oil
- ½ cup mozzarella cheese, grated

Method:

1. Combine all the ingredients.
2. Stir well.
3. Place mixture in the air fryer basket.
4. Set it to air fry.
5. Set temperature to 400 degrees F.
6. Cook for 30 minutes or until potatoes are tender enough.

Serving Suggestions: Sprinkle with grated Parmesan cheese.

Preparation & Cooking Tips: Use smoked paprika if available.

Chapter 3: Beef Recipes

Meatballs in Honey Garlic Sauce

Preparation Time: 10 minutes
Cooking Time: 20 minutes
Servings: 6

Ingredients:

Meatball

- 1 lb. frozen meatballs
- Cooking spray

Honey garlic sauce

- 3 tablespoons soy sauce
- ¼ cup honey
- 1 tablespoon butter
- 1 cup ketchup
- 3 cloves garlic, minced

Method:

1. Place meatballs in the air fryer basket.
2. Set to air fry.
3. Cook at 380 degrees F for 10 minutes, stirring once or twice.
4. In a pan over medium heat, simmer the honey garlic sauce ingredients for 10 minutes.
5. Toss meatballs in honey garlic sauce and serve.

Serving Suggestions: Garnish with chopped parsley.

Preparation & Cooking Tips: You can also make your own meatballs.

Rib Eye STEAK WITH Lemon Butter Sauce

Preparation Time: 20 minutes

Cooking Time: 12 minutes

Servings: 2

Ingredients:

Steak

- 2 rib eye steaks
- 2 tablespoons olive oil
- 1 tablespoon steak seasoning
- Salt and pepper to taste

Sauce

- 1 cup butter
- 2 tablespoons lemon juice
- 1 tablespoon lemon zest
- 3 tablespoons chives, chopped
- Salt and pepper to taste

Method:

1. Brush both sides of steaks with oil.
2. Season with steak seasoning, salt and pepper.
3. Add steaks to the air fryer basket.
4. Choose air fry setting.
5. Cook at 400 degrees F for 5 to 6 minutes per side.
6. Combine sauce ingredients in a bowl.
7. Cover and freeze.
8. Top the steaks with the frozen butter before serving.

Serving Suggestions: Garnish with herb sprigs.

Preparation & Cooking Tips: Let steaks sit at room temperature for 30 minutes before seasoning.

Teriyaki Beef Kebab

Preparation Time: 1 hour and 10 minutes
Cooking Time: 10 minutes
Servings: 4

Ingredients:

- 1 ½ lb. sirloin steak, sliced into cubes
- 1 onion, diced
- 1 cup cherry tomatoes
- 1 red bell pepper, chopped
- 1 cup teriyaki sauce

Method:

1. Thread steak and veggies onto skewers.
2. Brush all sides with teriyaki sauce.
3. Marinate for 1 hour.
4. Add to the air fryer basket.
5. Choose air fry setting.
6. Cook at 400 degrees F for 5 minutes per side.

Serving Suggestions: Serve with tzatziki sauce

Preparation & Cooking Tips: If using wooden skewers, soak first in water for 30 minutes before using.

Burgers with Pepper Jack Cheese

Preparation Time: 10 minutes
Cooking Time: 15 minutes
Servings: 2

Ingredients:

- 1 lb. ground beef
- ½ onion, minced
- 1 clove garlic, minced
- 1 tablespoon BBQ seasoning
- Salt and pepper to taste
- ½ cup pepper Jack cheese

Method:

1. Combine all ingredients except cheese in a bowl.
2. Form patties from the mixture.
3. Stuff cheese inside burger.
4. Add burger patties to the air fryer basket.
5. Select air fry function.
6. Cook at 350 degrees F for 5 to 7 minutes per side.

Serving Suggestions: Serve with mustard and hot sauce.

Preparation & Cooking Tips: You can make the patties ahead of time, wrap and freeze until ready to air fry.

Garlic Mustard Steak

Preparation Time: 10 minutes
Cooking Time: 10 minutes
Servings: 2

Ingredients:

- 2 sirloin steaks
- 1 clove garlic, minced
- 4 tablespoons vegetable oil
- 2 tablespoons Dijon mustard
- Salt and pepper to taste

Method:

1. Sprinkle steak with garlic.
2. In a bowl, mix oil, mustard, salt and pepper.
3. Brush both sides with this mixture.
4. Add steaks to the air fryer basket.
5. Select air fry setting.
6. Set temperature to 400 degrees F.
7. Cook for 4 to 5 minutes per side.

Serving Suggestions: Serve with mashed potatoes and gravy.

Preparation & Cooking Tips: If you want your steaks well done, internal temperature should be 160 degrees F.

Baked Beef Stew

Preparation Time: 20 minutes
Cooking Time: 50 minutes
Servings: 8

Ingredients:

- 14 oz. canned diced tomatoes
- 1 cup water
- 3 tablespoons tapioca
- 2 teaspoons sugar
- Salt and pepper to taste
- 2 lb. beef stew meat, sliced into cubes and sautéed
- 4 carrots, sliced and boiled
- 3 potatoes, sliced and boiled
- 2 ribs celery, sliced
- 1 onion, sliced
- 1 slice bread, sliced into cubes

Method:

1. Combine ingredients in an air fryer safe bowl.
2. Divide into 2 bowls if necessary.
3. Place bowl inside the air fryer basket.
4. Choose bake setting.
5. Cook at 375 degrees F for 50 minutes.

Serving Suggestions: Serve with crusty bread.

Preparation & Cooking Tips: Use quick-cooking tapioca.

Beef Curry

Preparation Time: 20 minutes
Cooking Time: 20 minutes
Servings: 6

Ingredients:

- 2 lb. beef, sliced into cubes
- ½ teaspoon ground allspice
- 1 teaspoon ground cardamom
- Salt to taste
- 1 tablespoon olive oil
- 2 onions, chopped
- 2 cloves garlic, minced
- 1 tablespoon ginger, minced
- ¾ cup plain Greek yogurt
- 1 teaspoon ground cumin
- 2 teaspoons curry powder

Method:

1. Season beef with spices and salt.
2. Add oil to a pan over medium heat.
3. Cook onion, garlic, ginger and beef until beef is browned on all sides.
4. In an air fryer safe bowl, mix the remaining ingredients.
5. Stir in the beef mixture.
6. Place bowl inside the air fryer basket.
7. Select bake function.
8. Cook at 400 degrees F for 20 minutes.

Serving Suggestions: Serve with hot rice.

Preparation & Cooking Tips: You can also slice beef into strips.

Coffee Beef Roast

Preparation Time: 15 minutes
Cooking Time: 30 minutes
Servings: 6

Ingredients:

- 2 teaspoons vegetable oil
- 1 beef sirloin, sliced into strips
- 1 ½ cups brewed coffee
- 1 ½ cups mushrooms, sliced
- 2 cloves garlic, minced
- ¼ cup green onions, chopped
- Salt and pepper to taste

Method:

1. Pour oil into a pan over medium heat.
2. Add beef and cook until tender and browned.
3. Transfer beef to the air fryer.
4. Set it to air fry.
5. Cook for 5 minutes per side.
6. Add the coffee, mushrooms, garlic and green onion to the air fryer.
7. Season with salt and pepper.
8. Set it to roast.
9. Cook at 400 degrees F for 20 minutes.

Serving Suggestions: Serve with potato salad.

Preparation & Cooking Tips: You can use liquid smoke for the sauce for extra flavor.

Broiled Sirloin Steak

Preparation Time: 20 minutes
Cooking Time: 20 minutes
Servings: 4

Ingredients:

- 1 teaspoon onion powder
- 1 teaspoon garlic powder
- ¼ teaspoon mustard
- 2 tablespoons lime juice
- ¼ teaspoon dried thyme
- ¼ teaspoon dried oregano
- 4 beef sirloin steaks (5 ounces each)
- 1 cup mushrooms, sliced

Method:

1. Mix herbs and spices in a bowl.
2. Rub mixture on both sides of steaks.
3. Add steaks to the air fryer basket.
4. Stir in mushrooms.
5. Set it to broil.
6. Broil for 5 to 7 minutes until internal temperature reads 160 degrees F.

Serving Suggestions: Garnish with chopped chives.

Preparation & Cooking Tips: You can also add sliced onions to the beef mixture.

Broiled Beef & Broccoli

Preparation Time: 15 minutes
Cooking Time: 30 minutes
Servings: 8

Ingredients:

- 2 ½ lb. flank steak, sliced
- ¼ cup soy sauce
- 2 tablespoons olive oil
- ¼ cup toasted sesame oil
- 3 cloves garlic, minced
- 1 tablespoon ginger, grated
- 1 tablespoon brown sugar
- 2 cups shiitake mushrooms, sliced in half
- 4 cups broccoli florets

Method:

1. Combine all the ingredients in an air fryer safe bowl.
2. Place inside the air fryer basket.
3. Set it to broil.
4. Cook at 375 degrees F 3 to 5 minutes per side.

Serving Suggestions: Sprinkle with white sesame seeds.

Preparation & Cooking Tips: Slice the steak across the grain.

Chapter 4: Pork Recipes

Pork Chops with Parmesan Cheese & Herbs

Preparation Time: 10 minutes
Cooking Time: 25 minutes
Servings: 4

Ingredients:

- 4 pork chops
- Salt and pepper to taste
- ½ cup all-purpose flour
- 2 eggs
- ¼ cup Parmesan Cheese, grated
- ¼ cup breadcrumbs
- ½ teaspoon garlic powder
- ½ teaspoon thyme
- ½ teaspoon oregano
- ½ teaspoon basil
- 1 teaspoon sugar
- Cooking spray

Method:

1. Sprinkle both sides of pork chops with salt and pepper.
2. Coat with flour.
3. Dip in egg.
4. In a bowl, mix the remaining ingredients.
5. Dredge pork chops with this mixture.
6. Spray with oil.
7. Add to the air fryer basket.
8. Choose air fry setting.
9. Cook at 360 degrees F for 15 minutes.

Serving Suggestions: Serve with garlic potatoes.

Preparation & Cooking Tips: Use bone-in pork chops.

Blackened Pork Chops

Preparation Time: 10 minutes
Cooking Time: 15 minutes
Servings: 4

Ingredients:

- 1 lb. pork loin

Spice mixture

- 1 teaspoon paprika
- 1 teaspoon dried thyme
- 1 teaspoon chili powder
- 1 teaspoon cayenne pepper
- 1 teaspoon garlic powder
- 1 teaspoon sugar
- Salt and pepper to taste

Method:

1. Mix all the spices in a bowl.
2. Cover both sides of pork with this mixture.
3. Add pork to the air fryer basket.
4. Set it to air fry.
5. Cook at 360 degrees F for 6 to 8 minutes per side.

Serving Suggestions: Serve with salad or vegetable side dish.

Preparation & Cooking Tips: You can also use pork chops for this recipe.

Barbecue Pork Chop

Preparation Time: 5 minutes
Cooking Time: 10 minutes
Servings: 4

Ingredients:

- 4 pork chops

Rub

- ½ teaspoon dried paprika
- ½ teaspoon chili powder
- 1 teaspoon garlic powder
- 1 tablespoon brown sugar
- 1 teaspoon ground cumin
- ½ teaspoon all spice
- ½ teaspoon dry mustard
- Salt and pepper to taste

Method:

1. Combine rub ingredients in a bowl.
2. Coat both sides of pork chops with this mixture.
3. Add pork chops to the air fryer basket.
4. Select air fry setting.
5. Cook at 400 degrees F for 5 minutes per side.

Serving Suggestions: Serve with corn salsa.

Preparation & Co oking Tips: Internal temperature should reach 145 degrees F.

Italian Sausage Bites

Preparation Time: 5 minutes
Cooking Time: 10 minutes
Servings: 4

Ingredients:

- 1 lb. Italian sausage, sliced into smaller pieces
- 2 tablespoons olive oil
- Italian seasoning

Method:

1. Coat sausages with oil and seasoning.
2. Add sausages to the air fryer basket.
3. Spray with oil.
4. Cook at 400 degrees F for 5 minutes per side.

Serving Suggestions: Serve with mustard and hot sauce.

Preparation & Cooking Tips: You can also use other types of sausages for this recipe.

Honey Garlic Pork Chops

Preparation Time: 5 minutes
Cooking Time: 15 minutes
Servings: 4

Ingredients:

- 4 pork chops
- Salt and pepper to taste
- 4 tablespoons olive oil
- 4 cloves garlic, minced
- 2 tablespoons sweet chili sauce
- 4 tablespoons lemon juice
- ½ cup honey

Method:

1. Sprinkle pork chops with salt and pepper.
2. Add to the air fryer basket.
3. Choose air fry setting.
4. Cook at 400 degrees F for 7 minutes per side.
5. In a pan over medium heat, add oil and cook garlic for 30 seconds.
6. Stir in the rest of the ingredients.
7. Simmer for 10 minutes.
8. Toss pork chops in sauce before serving.

Serving Suggestions: Garnish with crispy garlic chips.

Preparation & Cooking Tips: You can also slice pork into strips if you like.

Baked Pork Chops with Sauce

Preparation Time: 30 minutes
Cooking Time: 30 minutes
Servings: 2

Ingredients:

- 2 tablespoons butter
- 2 pork chops
- ¼ cup onion, chopped
- 2 tablespoons water
- ¼ cup maple syrup
- 1/8 teaspoon garlic powder
- 2 teaspoons Worcestershire sauce
- 1 tablespoon cider vinegar
- 1 teaspoon chili powder
- Salt and pepper to taste

Method:

1. In a pan over medium heat, add butter and cook pork chops until brown on both sides.
2. Mix remaining ingredients in a bowl.
3. Pour mixture into the air fryer basket.
4. Add pork chops and coat evenly with sauce.
5. Select bake setting.
6. Cook at 350 degrees F for 30 minutes.

Serving Suggestions: Let sit for 5 minutes before serving.

Preparation & Cooking Tips: Trim pork before preparing.

Baked Smothered Pork Chops

Preparation Time: 20 minutes
Cooking Time: 50 minutes
Servings: 6

Ingredients:

- 6 pork chops
- Salt and pepper to taste
- 2 tablespoons canola oil
- 10 oz. cream of mushroom soup
- 2/3 cup chicken broth
- 1 cup sour cream
- ¼ teaspoon dried rosemary
- ½ teaspoon ground ginger

Method:

1. Season pork chops with salt and pepper.
2. In a pan over medium heat, add oil and cook pork chops until browned on both sides.
3. In a bowl, combine the remaining ingredients.
4. Add mixture to the air fryer basket along with the pork. Stir well.
5. Choose bake setting.
6. Cook at 350 degrees F for 50 minutes.

Serving Suggestions: Garnish with herb sprigs.

Preparation & Cooking Tips: You can also use other cuts of pork for this recipe.

Broiled Pork Chops

Preparation Time: 20 minutes
Cooking Time: 10 minutes
Servings: 4

Ingredients:

- ¾ cup ketchup
- ¾ cup water
- 2 teaspoons brown sugar
- 1 tablespoon Worcestershire sauce
- ½ teaspoon paprika
- 2 tablespoons white vinegar
- 1/2 teaspoon chili powder
- Salt and pepper to taste
- 6 pork chops

Method:

1. Add all ingredients except pork chops to a pan over medium heat.
2. Bring to a boil and reduce heat to simmer for 5 minutes.
3. Add sauce and pork chops to the air fryer basket.
4. Set it to broil.
5. Broil at 400 degrees F for 3 to 5 minutes per side.

Serving Suggestions: Let sit for 5 minutes before serving.

Preparation & Cooking Tips: You can also use the bake setting but set time to 50 minutes.

Roast Pork with Potatoes

Preparation Time: 20 minutes
Cooking Time: 2 hours
Servings: 4

Ingredients:

- 1 packet onion soup mix
- 2 cloves garlic, minced
- 1 tablespoon dried rosemary
- Salt and pepper to taste
- 1 pork loin roast, sliced
- 2 lb. potatoes, sliced
- 1 ½ cup onions, sliced

Method:

1. Combine all the ingredients in a shallow baking pan.
2. Mix well.
3. Add to the air fryer basket.
4. Choose roast setting.
5. Cook at 325 degrees F for 2 hours.

Serving Suggestions: Serve with condiments of choice.

Preparation & Cooking Tips: Slice pork to fit the air fryer basket.

Honey Glazed Ham

Preparation Time: 10 minutes
Cooking Time: 30 minutes
Servings: 4

Ingredients:

- 8 slices ham
- 2 tablespoons honey

Method:

1. Add ham to the air fryer basket.
2. Pour honey over the ham.
3. Stir to coat evenly.
4. Select air fry function.
5. Cook at 350 degrees F for 15 minutes per side.

Serving Suggestions: Serve with crusty bread.

Preparation & Cooking Tips: You can also let ham sit for 30 minutes before air frying.

Chapter 5: Lamb Recipes

Lamb Chops with Garlic & Rosemary

Preparation Time: 1 hour and 10 minutes
Cooking Time: 10 minutes
Servings: 4

Ingredients:

- 2 tablespoons olive oil
- 4 cloves garlic, minced
- 1 tablespoons rosemary
- 2 tablespoons lemon juice
- 1 teaspoon lemon zest
- Salt and pepper to taste
- 1 lb. lamb chops

Method:

1. Combine all the ingredients except lamb chops.
2. Add chops to the mixture.
3. Marinate for 1 hour.
4. Transfer to the air fryer basket.
5. Select air fry setting.
6. Cook at 400 degrees F for 3 to 5 minutes per side.

Serving Suggestions: Serve with grilled vegetables.

Preparation & Cooking Tips: If frozen, let lamb chops come to room temperature before air frying.

Lamb Chops with Thyme & Rosemary

Preparation Time: 10 minutes
Cooking Time: 10 minutes
Servings: 4

Ingredients:

- 3 tablespoons olive oil
- 2 tablespoons thyme, minced
- 2 tablespoons rosemary, minced
- Salt and pepper to taste
- 4 lamb chops

Method:

1. Mix oil, herbs, salt and pepper in a bowl.
2. Brush both sides of lamb chops with mixture.
3. Place inside the air fryer basket.
4. Set it to air fry.
5. Cook at 400 degrees F for 5 minutes per side.

Serving Suggestions: Serve with fresh green salad.

Preparation & Cooking Tips: If you want your lamb chops well done, internal temperature should reach 155 degrees F.

Lamb Chops with Herbed Butter

Preparation Time: 1 hour and 10 minutes
Cooking Time: 12 minutes
Servings: 4

Ingredients:

- 2 tablespoons butter
- 1 teaspoon dried rosemary
- 1 teaspoon dried tarragon
- 1 teaspoon dried basil
- 8 lamb chops
- Salt and pepper to taste

Method:

1. In a bowl, mix butter and herbs.
2. Roll into a log.
3. Wrap log with plastic and freeze for 1 hour.
4. Season lamb chops with salt and pepper.
5. Add to the air fryer basket.
6. Select air fry setting.
7. Cook at 400 degrees F for 5 minutes per side.
8. Slice the frozen butter.
9. Add on top of the lamb.
10. Air fry for another 2 minutes.

Serving Suggestions: Garnish with fresh herb sprigs.

Preparation & Cooking Tips: You can also top with the butter after cooking.

Greek Lamb Chops

Preparation Time: 40 minutes
Cooking Time: 10 minutes
Servings: 4

Ingredients:

- ¼ cup olive oil
- ¼ cup lemon juice
- 2 cloves garlic, minced
- 2 teaspoons dried oregano
- Salt and pepper to taste
- 4 lamb chops

Method:

1. Mix oil, lemon juice, garlic, oregano, salt and pepper in a bowl.
2. Coat lamb chops with this mixture.
3. Marinate for 30 minutes.
4. Add lamb chops to the air fryer basket.
5. Select air fry setting.
6. Cook at 400 degrees F for 5 minutes per side.

Serving Suggestions: Serve with tomato and cucumber salad.

Preparation & Cooking Tips: You can also use chopped fresh oregano for this recipe.

Classic Rack of Lamb

Preparation Time: 10 minutes
Cooking Time: 20 minutes
Servings: 4

Ingredients:

- 4 tablespoons olive oil
- 2 cloves garlic, minced
- 1 tablespoon dried thyme
- 2 tablespoons dried rosemary
- Salt and pepper to taste
- 1 rack of lamb

Method:

1. Combine oil, garlic, herbs, salt and pepper in a bowl.
2. Brush all sides of lamb rack with this mixture.
3. Add the lamb rack inside the air fryer basket.
4. Cook at 360 degrees F for 10 minutes per side.

Serving Suggestions: Serve with steamed veggies.

Preparation & Cooking Tips: Slice the lamb to fit inside the air fryer basket.

New England Lamb Bake

Preparation Time: 30 minutes
Cooking Time: 50 minutes
Servings: 8

Ingredients:

- 1 tablespoon canola oil
- 1 onion, chopped
- 2 lb. leg of lamb, sliced into cubes
- ¼ cup all-purpose flour
- 3 cups chicken broth
- 2 leeks, chopped
- 3 potatoes, sliced
- 2 carrots, sliced
- 3 tablespoons butter
- ½ teaspoon dried rosemary
- ¼ teaspoon dried thyme
- 2 tablespoons parsley
- Salt and pepper to taste

Method:

1. Add oil to a pan over medium heat.
2. Add onion and lamb.
3. Cook until browned on all sides.
4. Stir in the flour and broth.
5. Bring to a boil.
6. Simmer for 3 minutes.
7. Add the rest of the ingredients.
8. Simmer for 10 minutes.
9. Transfer to the air fryer basket.
10. Select bake function.
11. Bake at 375 degrees F for 30 minutes.

Serving Suggestions: Garnish with additional parsley.

Preparation & Cooking Tips: Use boneless leg of lamb.

Broiled Lamb Chops

Preparation Time: 10 minutes
Cooking Time: 6 minutes
Servings: 4

Ingredients:

- 4 lamb chops
- 1 tablespoon olive oil
- 1 tablespoon soy sauce
- 1 teaspoon rosemary, chopped
- 2 cloves garlic, minced
- ½ cup red wine

Method:

1. Combine all the ingredients in a bowl.
2. Transfer to the air fryer basket.
3. Select broil setting.
4. Broil for 3 minutes per side.

Serving Suggestions: Garnish with herb sprigs.

Preparation & Cooking Tips: Trim fat from lamb before using.

Roast Lamb

Preparation Time: 20 minutes
Cooking Time: 1 hour and 20 minutes
Servings: 12

Ingredients:

- 1 leg of lamb
- 3 cloves garlic, sliced in half
- 1 teaspoon dried oregano
- Salt and pepper to taste
- 16 oz. tomato sauce
- 1 cup water
- 1 tablespoon lemon juice

Method:

1. Slice slits in the lamb leg.
2. Insert garlic cloves in the slits.
3. Rub all sides of leg with oregano, salt and pepper.
4. Place inside the air fryer basket.
5. Choose roast setting.
6. Cook at 400 degrees F for 30 minutes.
7. Reduce temperature to 350 degrees F.
8. Cook for another 50 minutes.

Serving Suggestions: Garnish with lemon wedges.

Preparation & Cooking Tips: Slice lamb to fit inside the air fryer basket.

Lamb Chops with Marjoram & Thyme

Preparation Time: 1 hour and 10 minutes
Cooking Time: 10 minutes
Servings: 4

Ingredients:

- 2 teaspoons dried thyme
- 1 teaspoon dried marjoram
- 1 teaspoon dried basil
- Salt and pepper to taste
- 4 lamb chops

Method:

1. Mix herbs, salt and pepper.
2. Rub mixture on all sides of lamb chops.
3. Marinate for 1 hour.
4. Place inside the air fryer basket.
5. Choose broil function.
6. Broil for 4 to 5 minutes per side.

Serving Suggestions: Serve with fresh green salad.

Preparation & Cooking Tips: Trim lamb before preparing.

Honey Glazed Lamb Chops

Preparation Time: 20 minutes
Cooking Time: 10 minutes
Servings: 4

Ingredients:

- ¼ cup honey
- ¼ cup mustard
- 1/8 teaspoon onion salt
- Pepper to taste
- 4 lamb chops

Method:

1. Add mustard, honey, salt and pepper in a pan over medium heat.
2. Cook while stirring for 2 minutes.
3. Brush both sides of lamb with mixture.
4. Place inside the air fryer basket.
5. Select broil setting.
6. Broil for 5 to 6 minutes per side.

Serving Suggestions: Drizzle with a little honey before serving.

Preparation & Cooking Tips: You can also use maple syrup instead of honey.

Chapter 6: Chicken Recipes

Chicken Bites

Preparation Time: 10 minutes
Cooking Time: 10 minutes
Servings: 4

Ingredients:

- 1 lb. ground chicken
- 1 bell pepper, minced
- 1 onion, minced
- Salt and pepper to taste

Method:

1. Combine all the ingredients in a bowl.
2. Mix well.
3. Form balls from the mixture.
4. Add chicken meatballs to the air fryer basket.
5. Select air fry setting.
6. Cook at 400 degrees F for 8 to 10 minutes, stirring from time to time to cook evenly.

Serving Suggestions: Toss in warmed barbecue sauce before serving.

Preparation & Cooking Tips: You can also use ground turkey if you like.

Chicken Parmesan

Preparation Time: 10 minutes
Cooking Time: 20 minutes
Servings: 4

Ingredients:

- 2 eggs, beaten
- 4 tablespoons vegetable oil
- 1 teaspoon Italian seasoning
- 3 tablespoons Parmesan cheese
- 1 cup breadcrumbs
- 4 chicken breast fillets
- 1 cup marinara sauce
- ½ cup mozzarella cheese, shredded

Method:

1. Add eggs to a bowl.
2. Add oil, seasoning, Parmesan cheese, and breadcrumbs to another bowl.
3. Dip chicken in eggs and dredge with breadcrumb mixture.
4. Add to the air fryer basket.
5. Set it to air fry.
6. Cook at 350 degrees F for 10 minutes per side.
7. Pour in marinara sauce and sprinkle cheese on top of the chicken.
8. Air fry for another 3 minutes.

Serving Suggestions: Sprinkle with dried basil before serving.

Preparation & Cooking Tips: Cook a little longer if fillet is thick.

Chicken Bang Bang

Preparation Time: 20 minutes
Cooking Time: 10 minutes
Servings: 6

Ingredients:

- 1 cup all-purpose flour
- Salt and pepper to taste
- 1 cup buttermilk
- 2 cups breadcrumbs
- 1 lb. chicken tenderloin, sliced into cubes
- ½ teaspoon hot pepper sauce
- ½ cup mayo
- ½ cup sweet chili sauce

Method:

1. Add flour, salt and pepper to a bowl.
2. Pour buttermilk into another bowl.
3. Place breadcrumbs to a third bowl.
4. Coat chicken with flour.
5. Dip in milk and dredge with breadcrumbs.
6. Place chicken in the air fryer basket.
7. Choose air fry setting.
8. Cook at 390 degrees F for 5 minutes per side.
9. Mix remaining ingredients in a bowl.
10. Toss chicken in sauce before serving.

Serving Suggestions: Garnish with green onion.

Preparation & Cooking Tips: You can also spray breaded chicken with oil before air frying.

Chicken with Tomatoes & Arugula

Preparation Time: 20 minutes
Cooking Time: 20 minutes
Servings: 2

Ingredients:

- 2 chicken breast fillets
- 3 tablespoons olive oil, divided
- 2 tablespoons chicken rub
- Salt and pepper to taste
- 1 cup arugula
- 1 cup cherry tomatoes

Method:

1. Coat chicken breasts with half of oil.
2. Season with chicken rub, salt and pepper.
3. Add to the air fryer basket.
4. Toss arugula and cherry tomatoes in the remaining oil.
5. Add these to the other air fryer basket.
6. Set temperature at 370 degrees.
7. Cook chicken for 4 minutes per side.
8. Cook arugula mixture for 4 minutes.
9. Serve chicken on top of arugula and tomatoes.

Serving Suggestions: Drizzle with a little bit of lemon juice.

Preparation & Cooking Tips: You can also slice chicken into strips to cook faster.

Szechuan Chicken

Preparation Time: 20 minutes
Cooking Time: 10 minutes
Servings: 2

Ingredients:

- 1 lb. chicken breast fillet, sliced into cubes
- ¼ cup cornstarch
- Cooking spray

Sauce

- 1 tablespoon brown sugar
- 1 tablespoon black bean sauce
- ¼ teaspoon garlic powder
- ¼ cup mayonnaise
- 1 teaspoon hoisin
- 2 teaspoon honey
- 1 teaspoon vinegar
- 1 teaspoon pepper

Method:

1. Coat chicken cubes with cornstarch and spray with oil.
2. Place these in the air fryer basket.
3. Choose air fry setting.
4. Cook at 350 degrees F for 4 minutes per side.
5. In a bowl, mix the sauce ingredients.
6. Toss chicken in sauce and serve.

Serving Suggestions: Garnish with sesame seeds.

Preparation & Cooking Tips: Use rice wine vinegar if available.

Garlic & Lemon Chicken

Preparation Time: 15 minutes
Cooking Time: 30 minutes
Servings: 6

Ingredients:

- ¼ cup milk
- ¼ cup Parmesan cheese, grated
- ½ cup breadcrumbs
- 2 tablespoons parsley, chopped
- Salt and pepper to taste
- 6 chicken breast fillets
- ¼ cup butter, melted
- 2 cloves garlic, minced
- 2 tablespoons lemon juice

Method:

1. Pour milk into a bowl.
2. In another bowl, mix Parmesan cheese, breadcrumbs, parsley, salt and pepper.
3. Dip chicken in milk.
4. Dredge with breadcrumb mixture.
5. Place chicken inside the air fryer basket.
6. Select air fry setting.
7. Cook at 375 degrees F for 4 to 5 minutes per side.
8. Mix the remaining ingredients in a bowl.
9. Pour over the chicken.
10. Select bake function.
11. Cook at 425 degrees F for 20 minutes.

Serving Suggestions: Sprinkle with paprika before serving.

Preparation & Cooking Tips: You can use dried parsley if fresh is not available.

Chicken Cordon Bleu

Preparation Time: 20 minutes
Cooking Time: 40 minutes
Servings: 6

Ingredients:

- 6 chicken breast fillets
- 1 teaspoon sage
- 6 slices ham
- 6 slices mozzarella cheese
- ½ cup breadcrumbs
- 2 tablespoons Parmesan cheese, grated
- 2 tablespoons fresh parsley, minced

Method:

1. Season chicken breast with sage.
2. Top with ham and cheese.
3. Roll and secure with a toothpick.
4. Mix remaining ingredients in a bowl.
5. Dredge chicken with breadcrumb mixture.
6. Place inside the air fryer.
7. Select air fry setting.
8. Air fry at 380 degrees F for 10 minutes per side or until golden.

Serving Suggestions: Serve with mashed potatoes and gravy.

Preparation & Cooking Tips: Use part-skim mozzarella cheese.

Butter Chicken with Herbs

Preparation Time: 10 minutes

Cooking Time: 1 hour

Servings: 8

Ingredients:

- ½ cup butter, sliced into cubes
- 2 tablespoons fresh parsley, chopped
- 4 tablespoons fresh rosemary, chopped
- 8 chicken legs
- Salt and pepper to taste

Method:

1. Add butter to a pan over medium heat.
2. Once melted, add herbs.
3. Season chicken with salt and pepper.
4. Add chicken to the air fryer basket.
5. Pour in the butter sauce.
6. Select bake setting.
7. Cook at 350 degrees F for 30 minutes per side.

Serving Suggestions: Serve with garlic roasted potatoes.

Preparation & Cooking Tips: Cook until internal temperature reaches 170 degrees F.

Baked Stuffed Chicken

Preparation Time: 20 minutes
Cooking Time: 50 minutes
Servings: 4

Ingredients:

- 4 chicken breast fillets
- Salt and pepper to taste
- ½ cup pesto
- ¾ cup mushrooms, chopped
- Cooking spray

Method:

1. Make a slit on top of the chicken breast.
2. Season with salt and pepper.
3. Stuff pocket with pesto and mushrooms.
4. Spray with oil.
5. Place inside the air fryer basket.
6. Choose bake setting.
7. Bake at 370 degrees F for 50 minutes, flipping once.

Serving Suggestions: Serve with fresh green salad.

Preparation & Cooking Tips: You can also add dried parsley to the mixture.

Mediterranean Chicken

Preparation Time: 20 minutes
Cooking Time: 20 minutes
Servings: 4

Ingredients:

- 4 chicken breast fillets
- Salt and pepper to taste
- 3 tablespoons olive oil
- 1 cup grape tomatoes
- 16 black olives, sliced
- 3 tablespoons capers

Method:

1. Season chicken with salt and pepper.
2. Add oil to a pan over medium heat.
3. Cook chicken for 3 minutes per side.
4. Stir in the remaining ingredients.
5. Cook for 3 minutes.
6. Transfer mixture to the air fryer basket.
7. Select bake setting.
8. Set it to 400 degrees F.
9. Bake for 10 minutes.

Serving Suggestions: Garnish with herb sprigs.

Preparation & Cooking Tips: You can also slice chicken into strips to cook faster.

Chapter 7: Fish Recipes

Tuna Steak

Preparation Time: 10 minutes
Cooking Time: 15 minutes
Servings: 4

Ingredients:

- 2 tablespoons olive oil
- 1 tablespoon lemon zest
- 2 tablespoons lemon juice
- 2 teaspoon dried thyme
- 2 cloves garlic, minced
- Salt and pepper to taste
- 4 tuna steaks

Method:

1. In a bowl, combine all ingredients except tuna steaks.
2. Add tuna to the bowl.
3. Marinate in the mixture for 30 minutes.
4. Add tuna to the air fryer basket.
5. Cook at 380 degrees F for 5 to 7 minutes per side.

Serving Suggestions: Garnish with lemon wedges.

Preparation & Cooking Tips: You can also use tilapia fillet for this recipe.

Coconut Crusted Tilapia

Preparation Time: 10 minutes
Cooking Time: 10 minutes
Servings: 4

Ingredients:

- ½ cup coconut flour
- 1 cup coconut flakes
- Salt to taste
- 3 eggs, beaten
- 4 tilapia fillets

Method:

1. Mix flour, coconut flakes and salt in a bowl.
2. Add eggs to another bowl.
3. Dip fish in the eggs and then dredge with coconut mixture.
4. Add fish to the air fryer basket.
5. Set it to air fry.
6. Cook at 400 degrees F for 4 to 5 minutes per side.

Serving Suggestions: Serve with spicy mayo sauce.

Preparation & Cooking Tips: Use unsweetened coconut flakes.

Baked Salmon in Honey Lemon Sauce

Preparation Time: 10 minutes
Cooking Time: 30 minutes
Servings: 2

Ingredients:

- ½ cup butter, melted
- 4 tablespoons honey
- 3 tablespoons lemon juice
- Salt and pepper to taste
- 2 salmon fillets

Method:

1. Mix all the ingredients except fish in a bowl.
2. Brush both sides of fish with sauce.
3. Add to the air fryer basket.
4. Select bake setting.
5. Bake at 390 degrees F for 15 minutes per side.

Serving Suggestions: Garnish with lemon wedges.

Preparation & Cooking Tips: Check if fish is fully cooked.

Salmon in Lemon Mustard Sauce

Preparation Time: 10 minutes
Cooking Time: 20 minutes
Servings: 2

Ingredients:

- 2 tablespoons olive oil
- 2 cloves garlic, minced
- 2 tablespoons lemon juice
- 1 tablespoon mustard
- ½ teaspoon ground thyme
- Salt and pepper to taste
- 2 salmon fillets

Method:

1. Mix oil, garlic, lemon juice, mustard, thyme, salt and pepper in a bowl.
2. Brush both sides of salmon with this mixture.
3. Place salmon inside the air fryer basket.
4. Choose bake function.
5. Bake at 400 degrees F for 10 minutes per side.

Serving Suggestions: Garnish with thyme sprigs.

Preparation & Cooking Tips: Use Dijon mustard if available.

Beer-Battered Fish

Preparation Time: 30 minutes
Cooking Time: 12 minutes
Servings: 2

Ingredients:

- 2 cod fillets, sliced into strips
- Cooking spray

Batter

- 1 cup all-purpose flour
- 1 teaspoon baking soda
- 2 tablespoons cornstarch
- 8 oz. beer
- 1 egg
- Salt and pepper to taste

Flour mixture for dredging

- 1 cup all-purpose flour
- 1 teaspoon paprika
- 1 teaspoon garlic powder
- 1 teaspoon Old Bay seasoning

Method:

1. Combine the batter ingredients in a bowl.
2. In another bowl, mix the flour mixture ingredients.
3. Spray fish with oil.
4. Coat with batter and dredge with flour.
5. Add to the air fryer basket.
6. Select air fry setting.
7. Cook at 380 degrees F for 6 to 7 minutes per side.

Serving Suggestions: Garnish with lemon slices.

Preparation & Cooking Tips: Refrigerate batter for 1 hour before using.

Crispy Haddock

Preparation Time: 10 minutes
Cooking Time: 12 minutes
Servings: 4

Ingredients:

- ½ cup all-purpose flour
- 6 tablespoons mayonnaise
- 2 eggs
- 3 cups breadcrumbs
- Salt and pepper to taste
- 4 haddock fish fillets

Method:

1. Add flour to a bowl.
2. Mix mayo and egg in another bowl.
3. In the third bowl, mix breadcrumbs, salt and pepper.
4. Coat fish with flour.
5. Dip in mayo mixture and dredge with breadcrumb mixture.
6. Place in the air fryer basket.
7. Set it to air fry.
8. Cook at 350 degrees F for 4 to 6 minutes per side.

Serving Suggestions: Serve with tartar sauce.

Preparation & Cooking Tips: Check if fish is flaky as this means that it is already done.

Salmon Patties

Preparation Time: 10 minutes
Cooking Time: 10 minutes
Servings: 4

Ingredients:

- 15 oz. salmon flakes
- 1 egg, beaten
- ¼ cup onion, chopped
- ½ cup breadcrumbs
- 1 teaspoon dill weed
- Salt and pepper to taste

Method:

1. Mix all the ingredients in a bowl.
2. Shape mixture into 4 patties.
3. Place 2 patties in 1 air fryer basket and 2 patties in the other air fryer basket.
4. Select air fry setting.
5. Set temperature to 370 degrees F.
6. Cook for 5 minutes per side.

Serving Suggestions: Serve with garlic mayo dip.

Preparation & Cooking Tips: Squeeze fish dry with paper towels before using.

Lemon & Herb Roasted Salmon

Preparation Time: 10 minutes
Cooking Time: 10 minutes
Servings: 2

Ingredients:

- 2 tablespoons butter, melted
- 2 cloves garlic, minced
- 1 teaspoon Italian seasoning mix
- ½ teaspoon red pepper flakes
- Salt and pepper to taste
- 1 tablespoon lemon juice
- 1 teaspoon lemon zest
- 2 salmon fillets

Method:

1. Combine all the ingredients except salmon fillets in a bowl.
2. Coat salmon with the butter mixture.
3. Transfer to the air fryer basket.
4. Choose air fry setting.
5. Cook at 400 degrees F for 10 minutes per side.

Serving Suggestions: Garnish with lemon wedges.

Preparation & Cooking Tips: You can also use tuna steak for this recipe.

Swordfish Fillet with Mango Salsa

Preparation Time: 10 minutes
Cooking Time: 10 minutes
Servings: 4

Ingredients:

- 4 swordfish steaks
- Salt and pepper to taste

Salsa

- 2 mangoes, sliced into cubes
- ½ cup red onion, chopped
- 1 jalapeno pepper, diced
- ½ cup cilantro, sliced
- 2 tablespoons lime juice

Method:

1. Sprinkle both sides of fish with salt and pepper.
2. Let sit for 5 minutes.
3. Add fish to the air fryer basket.
4. Select roast setting.
5. Cook at 400 degrees F for 5 minutes per side.
6. Mix salsa ingredients in a bowl.
7. Top fish with salsa and serve.

Serving Suggestions: Serve with fish sauce and vinegar.

Preparation & Cooking Tips: You can also make tomato salsa instead of mango salsa.

Cod with Creamy Garlic Pesto Sauce

Preparation Time: 10 minutes
Cooking Time: 15 minutes
Servings: 4

Ingredients:

- 4 cod fillets
- 1 tablespoon olive oil
- 2 cloves garlic, minced
- ¼ cup basil pesto
- 3 tablespoons cream
- Salt and pepper to taste

Method:

1. Add oil to a pan over medium heat.
2. Cook garlic for 30 seconds, stirring frequently.
3. Stir in the remaining ingredients except fish.
4. Simmer for 5 minutes. Set aside.
5. Season fish with salt and pepper.
6. Add fish to the air fryer basket.
7. Set it to air fry.
8. Cook at 350 degrees F for 5 minutes per side.
9. Pour sauce over the fish and serve.

Serving Suggestions: Sprinkle crispy garlic chips on top.

Preparation & Cooking Tips: You can also spread sauce over the fish and bake in the air fryer for 5 minutes.

Chapter 8: Shrimp Recipes

Crispy Breaded Shrimp

Preparation Time: 10 minutes
Cooking Time: 10 minutes
Servings: 6

Ingredients:

- 1 lb. shrimp, peeled and deveined
- 2 eggs
- 1 onion, diced
- 1 teaspoon garlic powder
- 1 teaspoon ginger, minced
- ½ cup breadcrumbs
- Pepper to taste

Method:

1. Add eggs to a bowl.
2. Dip shrimp in eggs.
3. Combine remaining ingredients in another bowl.
4. Cover shrimp with this mixture.
5. Place in the air fryer basket.
6. Select air fry setting.
7. Cook at 350 degrees F for 5 minutes per side.

Serving Suggestions: Sprinkle with green onions.

Preparation & Cooking Tips: You can also use frozen shrimp but thaw first before using.

Shrimp with Creamy Garlic Butter Sauce

Preparation Time: 20 minutes
Cooking Time: 20 minutes
Servings: 4

Ingredients:

- 1 lb. shrimp
- 2 tablespoons olive oil
- 1 teaspoon garlic powder
- 1 teaspoon Italian seasoning

Sauce

- 3 tablespoons butter
- 2 cloves garlic, minced
- ¼ cup Parmesan cheese, grated
- 1 teaspoon Italian seasoning
- ½ cup chicken broth
- ¾ cup heavy cream

Method:

1. Toss shrimp in oil, garlic powder and Italian herbs.
2. Air fry at 400 degrees F for 5 minutes, flipping once.
3. In a bowl, mix the sauce ingredients.
4. Add sauce to the air fryer basket.
5. Select bake function.
6. Bake at 400 degrees F for 5 minutes.

Serving Suggestions: Garnish with chopped parsley.

Preparation & Cooking Tips: Use unsalted butter for the sauce.

Spicy Shrimp

Preparation Time: 10 minutes
Cooking Time: 10 minutes
Servings: 4

Ingredients:

- 2 lb. shrimp, peeled and deveined
- 1 teaspoon chili powder
- 1 teaspoon hot pepper sauce
- 1 teaspoon sugar
- 1 teaspoon smoked paprika
- 1 teaspoon ground cumin
- 1 teaspoon garlic powder
- 1 tablespoon lemon juice
- 2 tablespoons Worcestershire sauce
- Salt and pepper to taste

Method:

1. Combine all the ingredients in a large bowl.
2. Add to the air fryer basket.
3. Select bake function.
4. Cook at 400 degrees F for 4 to 5 minutes per side.

Serving Suggestions: Serve with grilled corn.

Preparation & Cooking Tips: Add liquid smoke to the mixture and use ancho chili powder if available.

Blackened Shrimp

Preparation Time: 10 minutes
Cooking Time: 10 minutes
Servings: 4

Ingredients:

- 2 tablespoons olive oil
- 1 clove garlic, minced
- 2 teaspoon paprika
- 1 teaspoon onion powder
- ¼ teaspoon cayenne pepper
- ½ teaspoon dried oregano
- ½ teaspoon dried thyme
- Salt and pepper to taste
- 1 lb. shrimp

Method:

1. Mix oil, garlic, herbs, spices, salt and pepper in a bowl.
2. Stir in the shrimp.
3. Transfer seasoned shrimp in the air fryer basket.
4. Choose air fry setting.
5. Cook at 400 degrees F for 6 minutes per side.

Serving Suggestions: Serve with cucumber salad.

Preparation & Cooking Tips: You can also marinate shrimp in spices for 30 minutes before air frying.

Lemon Pepper Shrimp

Preparation Time: 5 minutes
Cooking Time: 10 minutes
Servings: 2

Ingredients:

- 1 lb. shrimp, peeled and deveined
- 4 tablespoons olive oil
- 1 tablespoon lemon juice
- Salt and pepper to taste
- 2 cloves garlic, minced

Method:

1. Toss shrimp in oil and lemon juice.
2. Season with salt and pepper.
3. Sprinkle with garlic.
4. Transfer to the air fryer basket.
5. Select bake function.
6. Cook at 400 degrees F for 5 minutes per side.

Serving Suggestions: Serve with mustard and hot sauce.

Preparation & Cooking Tips: Once shrimp turns opaque, it means that it is already done.

Shrimp Scampi

Preparation Time: 10 minutes
Cooking Time: 20 minutes
Servings: 4

Ingredients:

Shrimp

- 2 lb. shrimp, peeled and deveined
- 1 ½ tablespoons olive oil
- 2 tablespoons lemon juice
- Salt and pepper to taste

Topping

- ¼ cup butter, melted
- 1 egg yolk
- ¼ cup shallots, diced
- 2 cloves garlic, minced
- 1 tablespoon Italian seasoning
- ¼ cup breadcrumbs

Method:

1. Combine shrimp ingredients in a bowl.
2. Add to the air fryer basket as the bottom layer.
3. Mix the topping ingredients in another bowl.
4. Spread on top of the shrimp.
5. Select bake setting.
6. Cook at 330 degrees F for 20 minutes.

Serving Suggestions: Sprinkle with pepper before serving.

Preparation & Cooking Tips: You can also toast breadcrumbs first before adding to the topping mixture.

Sweet & Sour Shrimp

Preparation Time: 5 minutes
Cooking Time: 5 minutes
Servings: 4

Ingredients:

- 1 lb. shrimp, peeled and deveined
- ½ cup sweet and sour sauce

Method:

1. Toss shrimp in sweet and sour sauce.
2. Add to the air fryer basket.
3. Choose air fry setting.
4. Cook at 400 degrees F for 5 minutes, flipping once.

Serving Suggestions: Garnish with sesame seeds and chopped green onion.

Preparation & Cooking Tips: Remove from air fryer once shrimp is opaque. Do not overcook.

Basil Shrimp

Preparation Time: 5 minutes
Cooking Time: 10 minutes
Servings: 4

Ingredients:

- 2 tablespoons olive oil
- 1 lb. shrimp, peeled and deveined
- 1 clove garlic, minced
- ¼ cup basil, chopped
- ½ cup Thai stir fry sauce

Method:

1. Combine all the ingredients in a bowl.
2. Transfer to the air fryer basket.
3. Set air fryer to bake function.
4. Cook at 350 degrees F for 10 minutes, stirring once.

Serving Suggestions: Serve with steamed green beans and hot rice.

Preparation & Cooking Tips: Use Thai basil if available.

Creamy Garlic Shrimp with Parmesan

Preparation Time: 5 minutes
Cooking Time: 5 minutes
Servings: 4

Ingredients:

- 2 lb. shrimp, peeled and deveined
- ½ cup creamy garlic herb dressing
- 2 tablespoons lemon juice
- 2 cloves garlic, minced
- 2 oz. Parmesan cheese, grated

Method:

1. Spread shrimp in the air fryer basket.
2. Select air fry setting.
3. Cook at 400 degrees F for 3 minutes per side.
4. Stir in the remaining ingredients.
5. Air fry for another 2 minutes.

Serving Suggestions: Serve with vegetable side dish.

Preparation & Cooking Tips: Use low-sodium dressing.

Coconut Shrimp

Preparation Time: 10 minutes
Cooking Time: 6 minutes
Servings: 6

Ingredients:

- 1 lb. shrimp, peeled and deveined
- Salt and pepper to taste
- ½ cup all-purpose flour
- 2 eggs
- ¼ cup breadcrumbs
- 1 cup coconut flakes
- Cooking spray

Method:

1. Season shrimp with salt and pepper.
2. Coat with flour and dip in egg.
3. Mix breadcrumbs and coconut flakes.
4. Dredge shrimp with this mixture.
5. Spray with oil.
6. Add to the air fryer basket.
7. Select air fry setting.
8. Cook at 400 degrees F for 3 minutes per side.

Serving Suggestions: Sprinkle coconut flakes on top.

Preparation & Cooking Tips: Use unsweetened coconut flakes.

Chapter 9: Vegetable Recipes

Baked Zucchini

Preparation Time: 10 minutes
Cooking Time: 20 minutes
Servings: 4

Ingredients:

- 1 tablespoon olive oil
- 1 zucchini, diced
- ½ cup breadcrumbs
- ¼ cup Parmesan cheese, grated
- 2 teaspoons dried thyme
- Cooking spray

Method:

1. Combine all the ingredients in a bowl.
2. Transfer to the air fryer basket.
3. Select bake function.
4. Bake at 250 degrees F for 20 to 30 minutes or until tender.

Serving Suggestions: Sprinkle Parmesan cheese on top before serving.

Preparation & Cooking Tips: Check the middle part of the casserole to see if tender.

Lemon Butter Green Beans

Preparation Time: 10 minutes
Cooking Time: 15 minutes
Servings: 6

Ingredients:

- 1 lb. green beans, sliced
- 2 tablespoons olive oil
- 2 cloves garlic, minced
- 2 tablespoons lemon juice
- 1 tablespoon Parmesan cheese
- 2 tablespoons butter

Method:

1. Add green beans to the air fryer.
2. Select air fry setting.
3. Cook at 390 degrees F for 10 minutes, stirring once or twice.
4. In a pan over medium heat, add butter and cook garlic for 30 seconds.
5. Stir in the rest of the ingredients.
6. Cook for 1 minute.
7. Pour sauce over the green beans and serve.

Serving Suggestions: Garnish with lemon wedges.

Preparation & Cooking Tips: Trim green beans before slicing.

Onion Rings

Preparation Time: 20 minutes
Cooking Time: 10 minutes
Servings: 6

Ingredients:

- 1 cup flour
- Salt and pepper to taste
- 1 egg, beaten
- 1 cup buttermilk
- 1 tablespoon Parmesan cheese
- ½ cup breadcrumbs
- 2 onions, sliced into rings
- Cooking spray

Method:

1. Add flour, salt and pepper to a bowl.
2. In another bowl, mix egg and buttermilk.
3. Combine Parmesan cheese and breadcrumbs to another bowl.
4. Coat onion rings with flour, dip in egg and dredge with breadcrumb mixture.
5. Spray with oil.
6. Add to the air fryer basket.
7. Set it to air fry.
8. Cook at 400 degrees F for 5 minutes per side.

Serving Suggestions: Serve with tartar sauce.

Preparation & Cooking Tips: You can also use frozen onion rings to save time.

Roasted Brussels Sprouts

Preparation Time: 10 minutes
Cooking Time: 15 minutes
Servings: 4

Ingredients:

- 1 lb. Brussels sprouts
- 1 tablespoon olive oil
- 1 teaspoon garlic salt
- Pepper to taste

Method:

1. Toss Brussels sprouts in olive oil.
2. Season with garlic salt and pepper.
3. Transfer to the air fryer basket.
4. Cook at 390 degrees F for 5 to 7 minutes per side.

Serving Suggestions: Sprinkle with crispy garlic bits or crispy bacon on top.

Preparation & Cooking Tips: You can also use minced garlic instead of garlic salt.

Buffalo Cauliflower

Preparation Time: 20 minutes
Cooking Time: 15 minutes
Servings: 6

Ingredients:

Cauliflower

- 1 head cauliflower, sliced into florets
- 1 tablespoon olive oil

Buffalo sauce

- ¼ teaspoon cumin
- ¼ teaspoon garlic powder
- ½ teaspoon paprika
- ¼ teaspoon dry mustard
- ¼ teaspoon cayenne pepper
- 3 cloves garlic, minced
- 4 tablespoons butter
- 2 tablespoons lime juice
- 1 cup hot pepper sauce
- Pepper to taste

Method:

1. Toss cauliflower in olive oil.
2. Add to the air fryer basket.
3. Choose roast setting.
4. Cook at 400 degrees F for 7 minutes, stirring once or twice.
5. Mix buffalo sauce ingredients in a bowl.
6. Toss cauliflower in sauce.
7. Air fry for another 5 minutes.

Serving Suggestions: Serve with blue cheese dressing.

Preparation & Cooking Tips: Use smoked paprika if available.

Honey Roasted Carrots

Preparation Time: 10 minutes
Cooking Time: 20 minutes
Servings: 4

Ingredients:

- 3 cups baby carrots
- 1 tablespoon olive oil
- 1 tablespoon honey
- Salt and pepper to taste

Method:

1. Toss carrots in oil.
2. Drizzle with honey and sprinkle with salt and pepper.
3. Add to the air fryer basket.
4. Choose roast setting.
5. Cook at 390 degrees F for 20 minutes, stirring once.

Serving Suggestions: Sprinkle with dill before serving.

Preparation & Cooking Tips: Maple syrup can be used in place of honey.

Parmesan Pickle Chips

Preparation Time: 10 minutes
Cooking Time: 10 minutes
Servings: 4

Ingredients:

- ¼ teaspoon dill weed
- ¼ cup Parmesan cheese
- ¼ cup breadcrumbs
- 2 eggs
- 1 jar dill pickles

Method:

1. Mix dill weed, Parmesan cheese and breadcrumbs in a bowl.
2. Beat eggs in another bowl.
3. Dip each dill pickle in the bowl with eggs.
4. Dredge with breadcrumb mixture.
5. Add to the air fryer basket.
6. Set it to air fry.
7. Cook at 390 degrees F for 4 to 5 minutes per side.

Serving Suggestions: Serve with dip of choice.

Preparation & Cooking Tips: Dry pickles with paper towels before coating with breadcrumbs.

Roasted Cabbage

Preparation Time: 10 minutes
Cooking Time: 8 minutes
Servings: 4

Ingredients:

- 1 head cabbage, sliced into quarters
- 1 tablespoon olive oil
- 1 teaspoon garlic powder
- 1 teaspoon red pepper flakes
- Salt and pepper to taste

Method:

1. Toss cabbage in olive oil.
2. Sprinkle with garlic powder, red pepper flakes, salt and pepper.
3. Add to the air fryer basket.
4. Select roast setting.
5. Cook at 350 degrees F for 4 minutes per side.

Serving Suggestions: Serve as side dish to grilled meat.

Preparation & Cooking Tips: Use roasted red pepper flakes if possible.

Bacon & Cheese Corn

Preparation Time: 10 minutes
Cooking Time: 12 minutes
Servings: 4

Ingredients:

- 4 ears corn, sliced into 4
- ¼ cup butter, melted
- ½ ranch dressing mix
- 1 cup cheddar cheese, shredded
- 3 slices bacon, cooked crisp and crumbled

Method:

1. Brush corn with butter.
2. Sprinkle with ranch dressing mix and cheese.
3. Add to the air fryer basket.
4. Set it to air fry.
5. Cook at 390 degrees F for 10 minutes, flipping once or twice.
6. Sprinkle cheese on top.
7. Cook for another 2 minutes.
8. Sprinkle with bacon before serving.

Serving Suggestions: Top with chopped parsley.

Preparation & Cooking Tips: You can also add herbs to the butter.

Garlic Mushrooms

Preparation Time: 10 minutes
Cooking Time: 10 minutes
Servings: 4

Ingredients:

- 8 oz. mushrooms
- 1 tablespoon olive oil
- 1 tablespoon butter, melted
- 1 teaspoon garlic powder
- 1 teaspoon Worcestershire Sauce
- Salt and pepper to taste

Method:

1. Mix all the ingredients in a bowl.
2. Transfer to the air fryer basket.
3. Choose air fry setting.
4. Cook at 400 degrees F for 3 to 5 minutes per side.

Serving Suggestions: Garnish with chopped parsley.

Preparation & Cooking Tips: You can also use garlic salt instead of garlic powder.

Chapter 10: Snack & Appetizer Recipes

Garlic Potato Wedges

Preparation Time: 10 minutes
Cooking Time: 15 minutes
Servings: 4

Ingredients:

- 2 large potatoes, sliced into wedges
- 2 tablespoons olive oil
- 2 teaspoons garlic powder

Method:

1. Toss potatoes in olive oil.
2. Sprinkle with garlic powder.
3. Add to the air fryer basket.
4. Cook at 390 degrees F for 15 minutes, flipping once or twice.

Serving Suggestions: Serve with ketchup and mayo.

Preparation & Cooking Tips: Use Russet potatoes if available.

Stuffed Mushrooms

Preparation Time: 10 minutes
Cooking Time: 15 minutes
Servings: 12

Ingredients:

- 4 tablespoons olive oil
- ½ cup breadcrumbs
- Salt and pepper to taste
- 12 mushroom caps, stemmed
- ¼ cup mozzarella cheese, shredded

Method:

1. Combine oil, breadcrumbs, salt and pepper in a bowl.
2. Top mushrooms with the mixture.
3. Add to the air fryer basket.
4. Set it to air fry.
5. Cook at 360 degrees F for 10 minutes.
6. Sprinkle cheese on top.
7. Air fry for another 5 minutes or until melted.

Serving Suggestions: Sprinkle with herbs.

Preparation & Cooking Tips: Use large mushrooms for this recipe.

Mozzarella Sticks

Preparation Time: 10 minutes
Cooking Time: 15 minutes
Servings: 16

Ingredients:

- 8 mozzarella sticks, sliced in half
- 1/2 cup flour
- 1 egg, beaten
- 1 teaspoon Italian Seasoning
- ¼ cup breadcrumbs

Method:

1. Cover mozzarella sticks with flour.
2. Dip in egg.
3. Mix breadcrumbs and Italian herbs.
4. Dredge mozzarella sticks with this mixture.
5. Place inside the air fryer basket.
6. Select air fry function.
7. Cook at 390 degrees F for 5 to 7 minutes per side or until golden.

Serving Suggestions: Serve with marinara sauce for dipping.

Preparation & Cooking Tips: Freeze mozzarella sticks before coating with breadcrumbs.

Empanada

Preparation Time: 20 minutes
Cooking Time: 20 minutes
Servings: 8

Ingredients:

- 1 lb. ground chicken
- 1 teaspoon sweet paprika
- 1 teaspoon ground cumin
- Salt and pepper to taste
- ½ cup cheddar cheese, shredded
- ½ cup tomato sauce
- 1 pack biscuit dough
- 1 egg white, beaten
- 2 tablespoons water

Method:

1. Brown ground chicken in a pan over medium heat.
2. Season with spices, salt and pepper.
3. Drain and transfer to a bowl.
4. Stir in tomato sauce.
5. Spread biscuit dough and slice into circles.
6. Add chicken mixture on top.
7. Fold and seal edges.
8. Mix egg and water.
9. Brush empanada with the egg mixture.
10. Add to the air fryer basket.
11. Select bake function.
12. Cook at 350 degrees F for 10 minutes per side.

Serving Suggestions: Let cool before serving.

Preparation & Cooking Tips: You can also add chopped carrots or potatoes to the chicken mixture.

Steak Fries

Preparation Time: 40 minutes
Cooking Time: 20 minutes
Servings: 6

Ingredients:

- 1 lb. potatoes, sliced into strips
- 1 tablespoon olive oil
- ½ teaspoon steak seasoning
- ½ tablespoon paprika
- 1 teaspoon garlic powder
- Salt and pepper to taste

Method:

1. Coat potatoes with oil.
2. Sprinkle with herbs and seasoning.
3. Transfer to the air fryer basket.
4. Select air fry setting.
5. Cook at 400 degrees F for 10 minutes.
6. Flip and cook for another 10 minutes.

Serving Suggestions: Serve with gravy and sprinkle with crispy bacon bits.

Preparation & Cooking Tips: Soak fries in cold water for 30 minutes before air frying to make sure fries are crispy.

Pull-Apart Pepperoni Pizza

Preparation Time: 20 minutes
Cooking Time: 30 minutes
Servings: 4

Ingredients:

- 1 pack biscuit dough, sliced into strips
- ½ cup pepperoni slices
- 1 cup pizza sauce
- 1 teaspoon olive oil
- 1 teaspoon garlic powder
- 1 teaspoon Italian seasoning
- 1 cup mozzarella cheese, shredded

Method:

1. Combine all the ingredients in a bowl.
2. Transfer to the air fryer basket.
3. Select bake setting.
4. Cook at 330 degrees F for 15 to 30 minutes or until golden.

Serving Suggestions: Sprinkle with Parmesan cheese before serving.

Preparation & Cooking Tips: Use low-sodium pizza sauce.

Waffle Fries

Preparation Time: 10 minutes
Cooking Time: 15 minutes
Servings: 4

Ingredients:

- 4 cups frozen waffle fries
- 1 cup cheddar cheese, shredded
- ¼ cup olives, sliced
- ½ cup salsa
- ½ cup sour cream

Method:

1. Arrange waffle fries inside the air fryer basket.
2. Select air fry setting.
3. Cook at 400 degrees F for 2 to 3 minutes per side.
4. Sprinkle cheese on top.
5. Choose bake function.
6. Cook for another 3 minutes.
7. Top with salsa and sour cream before serving.

Serving Suggestions: Sprinkle with crispy bacon bits.

Preparation & Cooking Tips: You can also serve or top with guacamole.

Herbed Ricotta & Veggie Dippers

Preparation Time: 10 minutes
Cooking Time: 10 minutes
Servings: 4

Ingredients:

- 15 oz. ricotta
- 2 eggs, beaten
- 3 tablespoons Parmesan cheese
- 2 teaspoon fresh rosemary, minced
- 1 tablespoon lemon zest
- Salt and pepper to taste
- Vegetable sticks (cucumber, carrots, zucchini)

Method:

1. Mix all the ingredients except vegetable strips.
2. Transfer to the air fryer basket.
3. Select air fry setting.
4. Cook at 380 degrees F for 10 minutes.

Serving Suggestions: Serve with nacho chips.

Preparation & Cooking Tips: Try to cook until surface turns golden.

Corn Fritters

Preparation Time: 10 minutes
Cooking Time: 10 minutes
Servings: 6

Ingredients:

- 1 ½ cup corn kernels
- 1 teaspoon sugar
- 1 egg, beaten
- ¼ cup milk
- 1/2 cup all-purpose flour
- ½ cup cheddar cheese, shredded
- 2 stalks green onions, chopped
- Salt and pepper to taste

Method:

1. Combine all the ingredients in a bowl.
2. Add 3 tablespoons in the air fryer baskets.
3. Set to air fry.
4. Cook at 350 degrees F for 5 minutes per side.
5. Repeat until batter is used up.

Serving Suggestions: Serve with sour cream.

Preparation & Cooking Tips: You can make corn fritters ahead of time, freeze and air fry when ready to serve.

Maple Roasted Cashews

Preparation Time: 5 minutes
Cooking Time: 10 minutes
Servings: 2

Ingredients:

- 1 cup raw cashews
- 2 tablespoons olive oil
- 2 teaspoon maple syrup

Method:

1. Toss cashews in oil.
2. Drizzle with maple syrup.
3. Place inside the air fryer basket.
4. Choose air fry function.
5. Cook at 370 degrees F for 10 minutes.

Serving Suggestions: Let cool and serve.

Preparation & Cooking Tips: Store in airtight jars for up to 3 days.

Chapter 11: Dessert Recipes

Chocolate Croissants

Preparation Time: 5 minutes
Cooking Time: 8 minutes
Servings: 8

Ingredients:

- 1 pack frozen croissant rolls
- ½ cup melted chocolate

Method:

1. Add croissant rolls to the air fryer basket.
2. Drizzle with chocolate.
3. Select air fry setting.
4. Cook at 320 degrees F for 4 minutes per side.

Serving Suggestions: Top with slivered almonds.

Preparation & Cooking Tips: You can also make your own croissant rolls if you like.

Cherry Pie

Preparation Time: 10 minutes
Cooking Time: 15 minutes
Servings: 2

Ingredients:

- 1 frozen pie crusts
- 10 oz. cherry filling
- 1 egg yolk, beaten
- 1 tablespoon milk

Method:

1. Slice pie crust in half.
2. Combine remaining ingredients.
3. Top pie crust with cherry mixture.
4. Fold and seal the edges.
5. Place inside the air fryer basket.
6. Choose air fry function.
7. Cook at 310 degrees F for 10 minutes.
8. Flip and cook for another 5 minutes.

Serving Suggestions: Let cool for 10 minutes before slicing and serving.

Preparation & Cooking Tips: Let frozen pie crusts come to room temperature for 10 minutes before using.

Coffee Cake

Preparation Time: 15 minutes
Cooking Time: 35 minutes
Servings: 6

Ingredients:

- 2 cups flour
- 2 teaspoons baking powder
- ¾ cup sugar
- ½ teaspoon salt
- ½ cup butter, melted
- 1 egg
- 1 teaspoon vanilla
- ¾ cup milk

Method:

1. In a bowl, combine dry ingredients.
2. Add wet ingredients to another bowl.
3. Add first bowl to the second one, stirring well.
4. Pour mixture into the air fryer basket.
5. Select bake setting.
6. Cook at 325 degrees F for 35 minutes.

Serving Suggestions: Top with whipped cream.

Preparation & Cooking Tips: Insert a toothpick in the center of the cake. If it comes out clean, it means it is clean.

Pumpkin Muffin

Preparation Time: 10 minutes
Cooking Time: 30 minutes
Servings: 6

Ingredients:

- 2 ¼ cup flour
- 1 teaspoon pumpkin pie spice
- 1 teaspoon baking soda
- ½ teaspoon salt
- 2 eggs, beaten
- 1 cup pumpkin puree
- ½ cup vegetable oil
- 2 cups sugar

Method:

1. In a large bowl, combine all the ingredients.
2. Add mixture to muffin cups.
3. Place muffin cups inside the air fryer basket.
4. Select bake function.
5. Cook at 320 degrees F for 20 to 30 minutes or until fully one.

Serving Suggestions: Top with whipped cream.

Preparation & Cooking Tips: Check frequently to avoid burning.

Apple Cobbler

Preparation Time: 10 minutes
Cooking Time: 15 minutes
Servings: 4

Ingredients:

Filling

- 4 apples, diced
- 2 tablespoons butter
- 1 cup sugar
- ½ teaspoon allspice
- ½ teaspoon nutmeg
- 1 teaspoon cinnamon
- ¼ cup water
- 1 teaspoon lemon juice
- 2 tablespoons cornstarch

Topping

- 1 cup Bisquick mix
- 2 tablespoons melted butter
- ¼ cup sugar
- ¼ cup milk

Method:

1. Combine the filling ingredients in a bowl.
2. Mix well.
3. Transfer to the air fryer basket.
4. In another bowl, mix the topping ingredients.
5. Spread a layer of topping on top of the apple mixture.
6. Select air fry setting.
7. Cook at 320 degrees F for 10 to 15 minutes.

Serving Suggestions: Serve with a cup of warm milk.

Preparation & Cooking Tips: You can also use nondairy milk for the topping mixture.

Banana Muffin

Preparation Time: 10 minutes
Cooking Time: 25 minutes
Servings: 8

Ingredients:

- 2 packs banana muffin mix
- 2 eggs, beaten
- 2/3 cup milk

Method:

1. Combine ingredients in a bowl.
2. Add to muffin cups.
3. Place muffin cups inside the air fryer basket.
4. Select bake setting.
5. Cook at 320 degrees F for 25 minutes.

Serving Suggestions: Top with whipped cream.

Preparation & Cooking Tips: Cook for 3 to 5 more minutes if not fully done.

Carrot Cake

Preparation Time: 10 minutes
Cooking Time: 15 minutes
Servings: 6

Ingredients:

- 1 carrot cake mix

Method:

1. Follow instructions for preparing carrot mix.
2. Pour batter into the air fryer basket.
3. Select air fry function.
4. Cook at 280 degrees F for 15 minutes.

Serving Suggestions: Top with cream cheese frosting.

Preparation & Cooking Tips: You can also mix your own carrot cake batter if you like.

Broiled Grapefruit

Preparation Time: 5 minutes
Cooking Time: 5 minutes
Servings: 4

Ingredients:

- 2 grapefruit, sliced in half
- 2 tablespoons brown sugar

Method:

1. Sprinkle grapefruit with sugar.
2. Add to the air fryer basket.
3. Set it to broil.
4. Cook for 5 minutes.

Serving Suggestions: Serve immediately.

Preparation & Cooking Tips: You can also drizzle with maple syrup.

Baked Apples

Preparation Time: 10 minutes
Cooking Time: 10 minutes
Servings: 1

Ingredients:

- 1 tablespoon butter
- 2 tablespoons raisins
- 2 tablespoons walnuts
- Pinch ground nutmeg
- 1 apple, sliced and cored

Method:

1. Combine all ingredients except apple.
2. Mix well.
3. Top apple with mixture.
4. Air fry at 350 degrees F for 20 minutes.

Preparation & Cooking Tips: You can also season with ground cinnamon.

Roasted Banana

Preparation Time: 10 minutes
Cooking Time: 10 minutes
Servings: 4

Ingredients:

- 4 bananas, sliced
- 1 tablespoon cinnamon powder
- 1 tablespoon olive oil

Method:

1. Mix ingredients in a bowl.
2. Add to the air fryer basket.
3. Select roast setting.
4. Cook at 350 degrees F for 3 minutes per side.

Serving Suggestions: Drizzle with honey.

Preparation & Cooking Tips: You can also use plantains for this recipe.

Conclusion

The Ninja Foodi DZ201 model lets you take advantage of the DualZone technology and cook more food quickly than regular air fryers or conventional cookers. Whip up two different foods and have them ready at the same time.

The Ninja Foodi 6-in-1 is equipped with an intuitive interface that makes it user-friendly. This also makes you want to use it more often. The non-stick coating of the crisper plates and baskets makes cleaning super easy to do. All these benefits allow you to enjoy the experience with the Ninja Foodi air fryer even more.

With a 10.7 percent compound annual growth rate, the global air fryer market is anticipated to become an industry that is worth 1.2 billion dollars in the next five years.

Ninja Foodi continues to push the boundaries with innovations in kitchen and home appliances that provide us with convenience.

These appliances are not only beautifully designed and competitively priced; they also offer new and exciting ways to carry out daily tasks.

Made in the USA
Middletown, DE
08 April 2022

63857356R00064